Wig is Wet!

illustrated by Paul Harvey

Scott Foresman

Editorial Offices: Glenview, Illinois • Parsippany, New Jersey • New York, New York
Sales Offices: Parsippany, New Jersey • Duluth, Georgia
Glenview, Illinois • Carrollton, Texas • Ontario, California

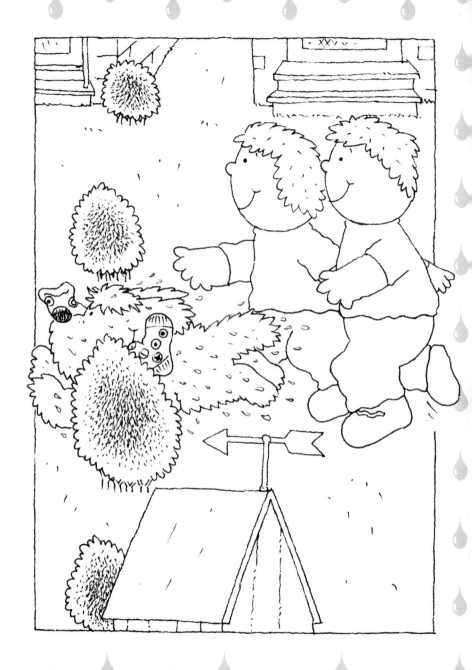